IMAGES

of America

HISTORIC
MILL CREEK PARK

The Suspension Bridge spanning Mill Creek was built by the Youngstown Bridge Company in 1895.

IMAGES

of America

HISTORIC
MILL CREEK PARK

Carol Potter and Rick Shale

ARCADIA
PUBLISHING

Published by Arcadia Publishing
Charleston, South Carolina

Library of Congress Catalog Card Number: 2005925972

For all general information contact Arcadia Publishing at:
Telephone 843-853-2070
Fax 843-853-0044
E-mail sales@arcadiapublishing.com
For customer service and orders:
Toll-Free 1-888-313-2665

Visit us on the Internet at www.arcadiapublishing.com

To my husband, John, who lives his life in rhythm with the land and its flora and fauna, cherishing the beauty of nature's intricate connections.
—Carol Potter

In memory of Don Shale (1912–1992) and Virginia Shale (1914–2004), who taught me to appreciate Mill Creek Park.
—Rick Shale

On the cover: Women pose at Lanterman's Falls at the dawn of the 20th century. (Courtesy of the Mahoning Valley Historical Society.)

CONTENTS

Acknowledgments   6

Introduction   7

1.   Volney Rogers and the Early Years   9

2.   Lanterman's Mill and Pioneer Pavilion   25

3.   The Waters of Mill Creek   37

4.   Bridges   55

5.   Vistas   65

6.   Structures and Attractions   75

7.   Recreation   91

8.   Fellows Riverside Gardens   119

ACKNOWLEDGMENTS

Grateful acknowledgment is made to the following individuals and institutions, which have contributed photographs to supplement the park's collection for this book: the *Vindicator* and Helen Paes and Robert McFerren; the Mahoning Valley Historical Society and Bill Lawson and Pam Speis; Mary Paolano Hoerner; the *Akron Beacon Journal* and Kimberly Barth; Scott Lanz; and Bill Whitehouse. Thanks to the assistance from the *Vindicator* and the Mahoning Valley Historical Society, this book offers a broader array of breathtaking, historic images of Mill Creek Park. The *Vindicator* was an early ally of the park's founder, Volney Rogers, supporting his dream to create Ohio's first park district. The Mahoning Valley Historical Society maintains archives of historic park documents and images. Always a great source for valley history, the historical society and its staff have enthusiastically encouraged Mill Creek Park's successful nomination for listing on the National Register of Historic Places. Landscape historian Mary Paolano Hoerner, the niece of landscape designer John Paolano, detailed her uncle's design philosophy for Fellows Riverside Gardens. The park's naturalist emeritus, Bill Whitehouse, sharing his wealth of park knowledge and experience, gave the authors rich material for captions. We are grateful for his help in telling the park's story. Landscape and architectural historian Rebecca M. Rogers was hired by the Mill Creek Park Foundation to write Mill Creek Park's nomination to the National Register of Historic Places. Her comprehensive nomination, the result of thorough research and dedication, was most useful for fact checking.

Most of all, we wish to thank park employees, commissioners, and volunteers—past and present—who have contributed their skills and talents to the incredible legacy of Volney Rogers, making Mill Creek MetroParks one of the most extraordinary preserved green spaces in America. You are quite a team and deserve to be recognized with proud appreciation.

Finally, we wish to acknowledge the support of our community and its recognition of the importance of Mill Creek Park.

INTRODUCTION

In 1891, Youngstown attorney Volney Rogers founded the first park district in Ohio: Mill Creek Park. Rogers possessed remarkable insights into the value of nature to the human condition. Rogers was motivated to offer an aesthetic and healthful alternative to the rapidly industrializing city of Youngstown with its unfiltered smokestacks, untreated drinking water, and crowded living conditions in the smoky environs of the Mahoning River.

Around 1890, after much exploration outside the city on horseback and on foot, Rogers decided that a section of land bordering Mill Creek should be set aside and protected from impending industrial development. Rogers had discovered the enchanting power of the hemlock-laced gorge area with its breathtaking Lanterman's Falls. His dream was to open this parcel of 400 acres to the people, enhancing the land and the lives of those who would visit there, partaking of nature's healing ways. Rogers wanted to share his discovery and preserve it for all future wanderers.

However, there was no legal instrument by which Rogers could achieve his dream. Writing the groundbreaking legislation to create a park district, he persuaded the Ohio legislature to pass an act authorizing the creation of a township park district. Youngstown voters approved the law, and in April 1891, Mill Creek Park was born. This road was to be a long, hard journey. The rugged character of the land, much of it adversely impacted by early industries and logging, presented great challenges to Rogers, already an astute planner, and the stellar group of landscape architects that he commissioned to plan one of America's most beautiful parks.

Volney Rogers became one of the first park commissioners and hired his brother Bruce to be the first park superintendent. He purchased land, persuading 196 landowners to sell, and worked with nationally prominent landscape architects Charles Eliot, H. W. S. Cleveland, and Warren H. Manning to design the park. Roads, bridges, and foot trails were constructed, and three dams were built to create pleasure lakes.

Once established, the benefits of Mill Creek Park were extraordinary. The falls and gorge areas were finally reclaimed after decades of refuse dumping. Forests were replanted, and the enchanting vistas for which the park is famous were groomed and opened to the appreciative gaze of Youngstown's citizenry. Woodlands and plantings helped to cleanse polluted air; Mill Creek flowed through the gorge—unobstructed and cleaner. Families not only had a destination for Sunday outings, but also the opportunity to build precious memories.

People flocked to Mill Creek Park. Softball leagues and picnics proliferated. Long walks and Sunday drives through a living cathedral enriched the lives of residents. The community developed a strong sense of ownership and pride in its unique public space as it earned its legendary claim as the most beautiful urban park in America.

The benefits of the land to people have increased over the last century. Recreation fields, golf courses, and trails are still great places of outdoor fun, spirits continue to soar with the great blue herons over the lakes, family gatherings abound at indoor and outdoor facilities, and educators work with folks of all ages—sharing the wonders of nature and horticulture. A magical garden draws visitors from around the world. The young and young at heart are charmed by a vast array of memorable special events.

Since voters approved converting to Mill Creek MetroParks in 1989, park lands have continued to enhance life in the community. There are new vistas to appreciate as more open space and its wildlife are protected from development. The legacy of Volney Rogers goes beyond the preserved and enhanced lands and waters; his lessons in stewardship travel home with every inspired visitor, giving support to those who strive to save our valuable environmental treasures. His philosophy was a century ahead of its time.

Pioneer Pavilion, constructed in 1821, was renovated in 1893 for public use, and an exterior staircase was added.

One

VOLNEY ROGERS AND
THE EARLY YEARS

As a member of the American Civic Association, Ohio attorney Volney Rogers participated in the 1883 conservation effort centered on Niagara Falls, a natural wonder threatened with development by electric companies. As legal counsel for the American Civic Association, Rogers argued that the diversion of water from the falls would destroy its beauty, something more valuable than the potential power. The American Civic Association's lobbying resulted in the establishment of Niagara Falls as New York's first state park in 1885. Rogers's success in this fight would place him in good stead for the battle in his adoptive home, Youngstown, for in this rapidly industrializing valley, a rare parcel of land was in great peril and in need of its own white knight.

Rogers devoted 30 years of his life to the improvement and protection of Mill Creek Park. He consulted the era's cutting-edge landscape architects: H. W. S. Cleveland of Minneapolis and Frederick Law Olmsted's disciples Charles Eliot and Warren H. Manning, both of Boston. Studying architecture, gardening, and urban planning, Rogers used his keen eye and intellect to guide park development.

Volney Rogers (1846–1919) founded
Mill Creek Park in 1891.

Raised on a farm in Columbiana County, Volney Rogers was the third of 11 children born to James and Elizabeth Jamieson Rogers. After completing school, Rogers worked as a teacher and a telegraph operator. While employed as a Pennsylvania legislature telegrapher, he decided to pursue a career in law. He was admitted to the bar in 1871, partnering with his brother Disney. Pictured here at a family reunion on July 4, 1915, are the following, from left to right: (first row) Volney, Disney, parents James and Elizabeth, Arminda, and Diogenes; (second row) James Jr., Lycurgus, Bruce, Zagonyi, and John.

This postcard reads, "On a sunny afternoon, listening to the music of the Falls at the Old Mill, Idora Park, Youngstown, Ohio." Idora Park was adjacent to Mill Creek Park but had no other connection. Early postcards often failed to correctly identify park locations. The confusion stems from the fact that Lanterman's Falls was once called Idora Falls. Passengers disembarking at the terminus of the streetcar line were within a few steps of both Idora and Mill Creek Parks.

Victorian ladies on an outing to Mill Creek Park pose on the rocks below Lanterman's Falls with the High Bridge that carried Canfield Road visible in the background. Climbing out to the rocks presented a challenge, especially when dressed in full-length skirts and high-buttoned boots. (Courtesy of the Mahoning Valley Historical Society.)

The Sulphur Spring was located on the eastern bank of Mill Creek between Lanterman's Falls and the Suspension Bridge on what is now the East Gorge Trail. Health enthusiasts started coming to the Sulphur Spring several years before the park's founding in 1891. Volney Rogers reported in the July 7, 1900, *Vindicator*: "My attention was first called to the spring by Dr. Timothy Woodbridge. He said that he frequently went to the place, and said it was fine water. He frequently drank the water and recommended it to his patients."

In the early years, the park's trails were called "rambles." Trails were designed features of the park that offered woodland settings and charming vistas. East Cohasset Ramble is the oldest trail in the park, predating the creation of Lake Cohasset (1897). Landscape architect Charles Eliot of Boston advised Volney Rogers on ways to enhance and stabilize the East Cohasset Ramble, which boasts fine hemlock stands and runs from Old Furnace Road to the Suspension Bridge.

Completed in 1897, Lake Cohasset was the first of the park's three artificial lakes. In 1894, Volney Rogers commissioned the nationally prominent engineer E. Sherman Gould of Yonkers, New York, to design a masonry dam for the proposed lake. The stone dam is visible at the far left. Early park vistas were created to capture the hemlock-lined waters. Boating began in 1898.

Umbrella Rock on the East Gorge Trail was a popular destination for sitting and experiencing the grandeur of the gorge. The Massillon sandstone formation was known as Cave Rock on an 1895 map. Rocks in the massive outcrop are over 250 million years old.

Many sites of early industry existed on lands that would later be acquired by the park. Shown here is Bears Den Quarry in 1897. William McKinley of Niles, Ohio, who later became the 25th president of the United States, was a key investor in the enterprise. The pole in the center of the photograph is a derrick that would hoist blocks of stone onto a rail car. The quarry yielded much of the sandstone used throughout the park for bridges, retaining walls, and structures. The quarry closed and was then reopened with Works Progress Administration labor in 1939–1940, closing finally in 1941. Remnants of the old quarry are visible today just west of Bears Den Cabin.

Another example of early industry on the banks of Mill Creek is ice harvesting, shown in this 1907 photograph. In the years prior to electrical refrigeration, Youngstown's ice was harvested from Mill Creek and the Mahoning River. The Youngstown Ice Company built an icehouse and dam a short distance downstream from the present Lake Glacier Dam at the confluence of Mill Creek and the Mahoning River, an area known as the Mill Creek Bottoms. Ice was cut in blocks by men with saws and hauled to storage buildings by horses. (Courtesy of the Mahoning Valley Historical Society.)

Skidding ice at Glacier Dam in 1907 was apparently less than a perfect art.

Mill Creek Park maintained its own police force, shown here about 1909, to preserve order and maintain safety for its guests. Police patrolled the grounds on foot, horseback, and bicycle. A report in the May 11, 1914, *Vindicator* broadly discusses attendance: "Mill Creek Park was the Mecca for thousands of people Sunday, the sunshine and warm weather serving to bring out a throng of people that filled the drives and paths all day long. Some people, principally in family groups, brought boxes and baskets of luncheon and stayed in the park all day, taking their al fresco meal in one of the thousands of shady nooks that dot the park. They came on foot, in autos and in street cars. . . . A veritable parade of vehicles rolled along the miles of roads that wind through the park, while only the immensity of the park prevented the pedestrians from crowding one another."

The Cohasset Swimming Club, a bathhouse located near Lake Cohasset, offered dressing rooms for ladies and gentlemen, along with restrooms, a veranda, and bathing suit rentals. As stated in the July 17, 1899, *Vindicator,* "The commissioners, agreeable to the request of many citizens, have decided to permit Sunday bathing for the accommodation of those who may be unable to visit the pool on week days." Two streetcar lines brought eager swimmers to the park.

Volney Rogers dedicated his life to the park, donating all of his legal services to the great cause. In 2000, he was inducted into the Ohio Natural Resources Hall of Fame, where his legend sits besides that of John Chapman (Johnny Appleseed). The entry reads, "Rogers played a pivotal role in establishing one of modern-day Ohio's great treasures—its local and metropolitan park districts—which provide millions of Ohioans with outdoor recreation and opportunities to appreciate nature. . . . He is best remembered for his personal efforts, against great odds, to preserve Mill Creek Park in Youngstown." (Courtesy of the Mahoning Valley Historical Society.)

The ritual of courting often occurred in Mill Creek Park, as the scenic trails provided young lovers with a degree of privacy.

Lover's Lane, Mill Creek Park, Youngstown, Ohio.

The Suspension Bridge is Mill Creek Park's oldest surviving span (built 1895) and the only extant steel bridge constructed by the Youngstown Bridge Company. Volney Rogers contracted with the company to build six bridges in the park: the Pine Hollow, Idora, Suspension, Slippery Rock, Cascade Ravine, and Old Orchard Bridges. Charles Fowler, chief engineer for the Youngstown Bridge Company, designed all of them. Shown here in 1918, the Suspension Bridge carries Valley Drive over Mill Creek. (Courtesy of the Mahoning Valley Historical Society.)

18

These young girls have gathered their armfuls of flowers at the Daisy Field. The exact location of the Daisy Field remains a mystery. (Courtesy of the Mahoning Valley Historical Society.)

A trail from Kiwatha Road leads south to the east side of Newport Dam. The ornamental dam railing is barely visible at the end of the trail.

This January 1945 view, looking north, shows the West Cohasset Trail.

The bathhouse on the east side of Lake Glacier offered swimmers changing rooms and bathing suit rentals. A second bathhouse was located on the west side at the north end of the lake. To cut costs, plans were made in 1921 to move all of the bathhouses to the west side of the lake, where there was a beach.

In 1916, a movie company came to Youngstown to produce the film *Vulcans of the Mahoning*, enlisting members of Youngstown's elite society as actors. The film starred Ysabelle Bonnell and John A. Logan III, pictured above on the running boards of a vehicle at the Suspension Bridge. Below, the cinematographer, using a hand-cranked motion picture camera, films the couple posing below the Lake Cohasset Dam as the director yells action into his megaphone. (Courtesy of the Mahoning Valley Historical Society.)

The Youngstown Chamber of Commerce formed a committee to honor Volney Rogers for his efforts in creating, planning, and protecting Mill Creek Park. Volney left for a tour of the West in February 1919. He stopped in Chicago to pose for sculptor Frederick C. Hibbard, who had been commissioned to create a bronze statue. In Colorado, Volney visited a site that resembled the Mill Creek Gorge and was caught in a surprise blizzard. He contracted a serious cold that led to pneumonia and his death on December 3, 1919, at the age of 73. Rogers is buried at Tod Cemetery in Youngstown.

VOLNEY ROGERS MEMORIAL,
ENTRANCE TO MILL CREEK PARK, YOUNGSTOWN, OHIO—12

VOLNEY
ROGERS
1848 1919

Volney Rogers's sad death was met with great mourning in Youngstown. Efforts progressed for a memorial to the remarkable man who had preserved a beautiful parcel of land for the enjoyment of all. Created by Chicago sculptor Frederick C. Hibbard, the eight-foot bronze statue stands on a pedestal of red Missouri marble. The tree in the sculpture is a dwarf white thorn, a species selected by Volney for its tenacity. The motto on the base reads, "This park was conceived in his heart and realized through his devotion."

Funds for the memorial, dedicated on October 12, 1920, came from public subscription, including donations from prominent citizens and Youngstown schoolchildren. The top subscription seller, Tad Fithian, and the winner of a Mill Creek Park essay contest, Ethel Rieser, had the honor of untying the ribbon binding the huge American flags. Schoolchildren then pulled the flags away with cords. At the ceremony, so many children jammed onto the speakers' stand that the railing collapsed; fortunately no one was hurt. (Courtesy of the *Vindicator*.)

Curator Edward Thomas of the Ohio State Historical Society wrote the following after the dedication: "If ever a man deserved a monument, it is Volney Rogers. He was the first to realize that Youngstown had a natural treasure that must be saved. He persevered through a tough but eventually successful fight and overcame the greatest of all obstacles—the apathy of the people. Because of his foresight and persistence and determination, Mill Creek Park is what it is today, instead of a dump for rubbish and tin cans. I wish that every Ohio City had a Volney Rogers and a Mill Creek Park."

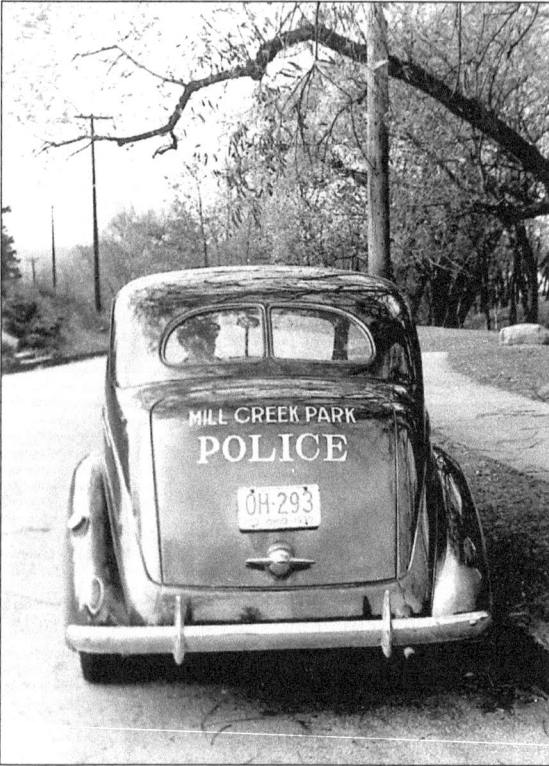

Police officer Don Brenner patrols Memorial Hill Drive in a newly lettered police car in November 1939.

Park commissioners Charles S. Robinson, Dr. Hugh Morgan, and James L. Wick Jr., shown left to right, served a total of 76 years. Under Morgan and Robinson, the park expanded from 400 acres to over 2,000. Robinson, an executive with Youngstown Sheet and Tube, was appointed to the Mill Creek Board on January 10, 1920, and served until his death on July 22, 1945. Morgan, a dentist, served from November 4, 1919, until his death on December 29, 1948. In the history of the park, no commissioner served longer than Morgan's 29-year tenure. Wick, a prominent industrial and civic leader, was president of the Falcon Bronze Company. He was appointed to the board on May 10, 1937, and served until August 4, 1958. The Wick Recreation Area is named in his honor.

Two

LANTERMAN'S MILL AND PIONEER PAVILION

Two of Mill Creek Park's favorite icons are Lanterman's Mill and Pioneer Pavilion, both of which predate the 1891 founding of the park. These buildings are among the most photographed places in the park and are also the focal points for numerous park trails. Both structures had nearby bridges by which the early settlers could cross Mill Creek. Lanterman's Mill, constructed in 1845–1846 by German Lanterman and Samuel Kimberly, and Pioneer Pavilion, built in 1821 as a woolen mill, are remnants of 19th-century industry, as well as splendid examples of adaptation for new uses.

Lanterman's Mill ceased operation in 1888, shortly before Volney Rogers purchased the property. In the late 19th and early 20th centuries, it was used for a bathhouse and storage, and in 1933, it was turned into a museum of natural history. In the 1980s, the building was restored to working order as a gristmill. Pioneer Pavilion evolved from a woolen mill to a blast furnace storage facility to a cattle barn and, finally, to the park's first party facility in 1893.

Lanterman's Mill is one of Mahoning County's most historic landmarks.

Two earlier mills preceded Lanterman's Mill. At the end of the 18th century, the land surrounding the falls belonged to John Young, founder of Youngstown. In August 1797, Young's surveyors, Isaac Powers and Phineas Hill, set out to explore the then unnamed Mill Creek. Coming upon the falls, the men immediately recognized the site's potential for a mill. Hill offered to purchase the 300 acres surrounding the falls. Young stipulated, as a condition of the sale, that Hill must build a saw- and gristmill on the site within 18 months of purchase. Around 1804, a covered bridge—the first of three spans to the mill—was built at a cost of $75. In 1823, a second mill replaced the original. Built by Eli Baldwin, this framed structure served only as a gristmill until 1843, when a flood washed it away.

This illustration shows the 19th-century covered bridge over Lanterman's Falls. Farmers from as far away as western Pennsylvania crossed the creek and gorge on this bridge to bring their loads of grain to the mill. The bridge served as the connector between the east and west sides of Mill Creek before the Canfield Road Bridge was built in 1883. The rural community also used the mill as an information hub, a spot where locals could advertise their wares and needs and catch up on local gossip. (Courtesy of the Mahoning Valley Historical Society.)

The current frame structure, the third mill at the site by Lanterman's Falls, was built in 1845–1846 by German Lanterman and his brother-in-law Samuel Kimberly and was used solely as a gristmill. German Lanterman was born in Austintown in 1814 and operated the mill from 1846 to 1888. It is believed that this mill was originally powered by an overshot wheel, the type presently being used, but was later converted to turbines prior to its 1888 closing. Lanterman's Mill was a highly successful operation, using three sets of grinding stones. Historians speculate that its downfall was due to the advent of roller mills, which were more efficient and less costly to run.

Amateur naturalist and professional photographer Frank Ferris stands in the Cave of the Winds under Lanterman's Falls in January 1948.

Subzero weather has produced a fully frozen Lanterman's Falls and giant icicles in the Cave of the Winds. (Courtesy of the *Vindicator*.)

After closing in 1888, the mill stood in a state of disrepair until purchased by the park in 1892. As an early park facility, the building held a ballroom, concession stand, and bathhouse for swimmers. Swimming continued in the Pool of Shadows until 1917. The upper floors of the mill were used for boat storage during the winter. The building was deteriorating rapidly, and the park renovated the infrastructure in 1915. In 1933, the first floor was converted into a nature museum, then into the park's historical museum in 1972.

Floodwaters race over Lanterman's Falls. (Courtesy of the *Vindicator*.)

Assistant naturalist Bill Whitehouse (left) and naturalist Lindley Vickers stand near the lip of Lanterman's Falls and peer at the diminished trickle of water caused by a severe period of low rainfall in August 1953. (Courtesy of the *Vindicator*.)

Bill Whitehouse, a 20-year-old assistant naturalist, works in the Old Mill Museum in the mid-1950s. During the years from 1933 to 1972, when the mill served as a nature museum, generations of area residents spent countless hours viewing mounted birds, mammals, and other natural history exhibits. Thousands of civic and school groups toured the mill before the park's nature education program shifted to the Ford Nature and Education Center in 1972. (Courtesy of the *Vindicator*.)

The renovation of Lanterman's Mill was no small feat. Many obstacles had to be overcome during the costly and painstaking renovation that began in 1982. Historical records and original blueprints of the mill were nonexistent. Dr. John White, professor of anthropology at Youngstown State University, organized an archeological dig that yielded valuable artifacts. Dr. White and his students contributed over 1,200 volunteer hours in their discovery of the location of the original millrace with original chestnut logs and a ledge that supported a waterwheel, which was notched into the stone foundation wall.

Expert gristmill renovators, Lorin Cameron and his sons Ed and Wayne of Damascus, Ohio, were commissioned to restore the structure to a working mill. The four-ton waterwheel was built off-site, marked piece by piece, disassembled, and rebuilt inside the mill.

The four grindstones had not been dressed or sharpened since the mill's closing in 1888. Transported across the Atlantic as ballast, two of the stones were made of French quartz. The second pair was made from solid granite called Virginia pebble. The park contacted the Society for the Preservation of Old Mills to find dressers skilled in the art of grooving millstones. Dressing is critical work, as poorly grooved wheels create sparks that can cause devastating mill explosions due to the volatility of fine grain dust in the air. In this photograph, Dewey Sheets of Indiana, age 89, inspects his handiwork while resurfacing grindstones. He and coworker James Lockard of Tennessee were in town to dress the stones. The completed, dressed wheels will now last through another century of grinding. (Courtesy of the *Vindicator*.)

After 90 years of park ownership, Lanterman's Mill operates again, grinding corn, oats, wheat, and buckwheat just as it did in the 19th century due to the generosity of the Beecher Foundations.

Pioneer Pavilion, one of the oldest structures in Youngstown, is a rare surviving example of early-19th-century industry. James Heaton constructed this sandstone building in 1821 as a mill for carding and fulling wool. A millrace from Mill Creek and a waterwheel on the west side supplied the power. In the 1830s and 1840s, the woolen mill was converted to a storage facility for the nearby Mill Creek Furnace and later served as a cattle barn.

Before this vista was obscured by tree growth, several features of the Pioneer Section of Mill Creek Park were visible: (left to right) the 1897 Lake Cohasset Dam, the curve of Old Furnace Road, and Pioneer Pavilion. West Cohasset Drive is at the top of the hill.

This postcard captures Pioneer Pavilion in winter. The steep hill on Old Furnace Road, shown at left, often presented a challenge for vehicles in snowy weather.

In 1891, Volney Rogers purchased this property for Mill Creek Park, renovated the building as a dining and dancing facility in 1893, and named it Pioneer Pavilion in honor of the region's pioneer forebears. The renovation was designed by Youngstown architect William B. Ellis. The elaborate stone staircase was added to the exterior in 1893. In the background is the original Old Furnace steel bridge, erected in 1885 and demolished in 1972.

During the renovation of Pioneer Pavilion, the third floor was removed to create a beautiful two-story ballroom. The unique molded mantle and fireplace feature an egg and dart design. The dramatic oak-beamed ballroom quickly became the area's premier location for reunions, parties, weddings, dances, and club meetings.

Youngstown ministers and their families gather on the ornately carved steps of Pioneer Pavilion. (Courtesy of the *Vindicator*.)

Three

THE WATERS OF
MILL CREEK

As the Mahoning River became fouled with waste from the iron and steel mills lining its shores, Mill Creek became in Volney Rogers's mind an alternative, a stream to be protected from industrial pollution. Named for the various mills its water powered, Mill Creek originates in Columbiana County and flows almost directly north for 20 miles until reaching the Mahoning River at the northern boundary of the park. Its most noted natural feature is Lanterman's Falls, where the creek drops two dozen feet into a broad pool.

Visitors to Mill Creek Park are often most impressed by three large bodies of water: Lakes Cohasset, Glacier, and Newport. When the park was formed in 1891, no lakes existed—except in Volney Rogers's imagination. Eventually, three dams were constructed across Mill Creek to create these artificial waters: Lake Cohasset in 1897, Lake Glacier in 1904–1905, and Lake Newport in 1928. Previously, the park commissioners had created two smaller bodies of water by damning Bear Creek: the Lily Pond and nearby Mirror Pond. These waters have provided scenic vistas and recreation such as swimming, boating, skating, and fishing for generations.

Climbing onto the huge rocks in Mill Creek to view the drama of the gorge was a favorite activity for the adventuresome. (Courtesy of the *Vindicator*.)

Volney's younger brother Bruce Rogers was Mill Creek Park's first superintendent, serving from 1891 to 1918. Pictured here pointing to the source of Mill Creek, he and geologist John H. Chase discovered the chief source of Mill Creek in Columbiana County about 20 miles south of Youngstown. Bruce, born in 1854, was asked by Volney to contribute his talents as a landscape architect and practical administrator. As a planner, Bruce directed much of the work of laying out the park. An amateur historian, he also helped to found the Youngstown McGuffey Society, honoring pioneer educator William Holmes McGuffey. Bruce was extremely loyal to achieving Volney's goals for the park.

The most dramatic natural feature of the Mill Creek watershed is Lanterman's Falls with its 23-foot drop. The Cave of the Winds is at the right. Lanterman's Falls has also been known as Mill Creek Falls, Baldwin Falls, and Idora Falls. Three gristmills have occupied the eastern side (left) of the falls.

The Lily Pond (also known as the Goldfish Pond), created in 1896 by damming a natural spring, became the park's first water attraction. H. W. S. Cleveland worked with Volney Rogers on plans for this area of the park. A foot trail encircles the four-acre pond, which has been one of the most popular spots in Mill Creek Park for over a century.

Generations of families have brought their young children to the Lily Pond to admire the ducks, geese, turtles, and fish. Lore tells of park police officer Martin Moran and the five goldfish he gave to Volney Rogers for release in the pond—the beginning of the water's goldfish population. Bass and bluegills lived among the masses of goldfish. Muskrats and sedimentation have been negative influences at the pond; the lily bulbs were consumed by muskrats, and huge silt accumulations had to be dredged in 1935 and again in 1975. (Courtesy of the *Vindicator*.)

Seen from the ridge near the old Fresh Air Camp on the former One-Way Drive, the Lily Pond and a portion of the foot trail encircling it sit within a tree-framed vista. The Frog Pond appears in the background. (Courtesy of the *Vindicator*.)

The Lily Pond is located within the oldest area of Mill Creek Park, the Pioneer Section, near the original 1936 Birch Hill Cabin. Birch Hill Cabin stands on the sandstone foundation of Volney Rogers's summerhouse, the Hermitage. The Lily Pond flows into the Frog Pond and then over an 11-foot spillway into Mirror Pond.

Lake Cohasset, the park's first artificial lake, was completed in 1898. The 28-acre body of water was part of the layout by Volney Rogers and H. W. S. Cleveland. Cohasset means "place of the hemlocks or pines" in the language of the Delaware Indians. In 1898, the park purchased the naphtha boat shown here from Lyman Brothers of Cleveland. Although the boat had only 30 seats, it was billed as accommodating 65 passengers. Round-trip fare for a ride the length of Lake Cohasset was 10¢ in 1898. The May 1898 *Vindicator* says of the boat, "No name was given the launch, and as this is a delicate matter on the part of Mr. Rogers, he will likely not apply the proper title, which by all means should be the *Volney Rogers*, as he has done so much toward beautifying the park and making the surroundings picturesque."

The Cohasset naphtha boat was eventually named the *Narama*. During the day, boat tours left on the half hour to coordinate with streetcar schedules. Moonlight parties on the scenic lake were also a favorite activity. An early boat landing on the east shore is visible at center.

Tucked into a protected shoreline of Lake Cohasset stands the old boat landing in April 1922. Records show that the price to rent boats in 1900 was 25¢ an hour for small boats and 30¢ for large boats.

The Lake Cohasset spillway was engineered to have a height of 23 feet and a width of 147 feet. (Courtesy of the *Vindicator*.)

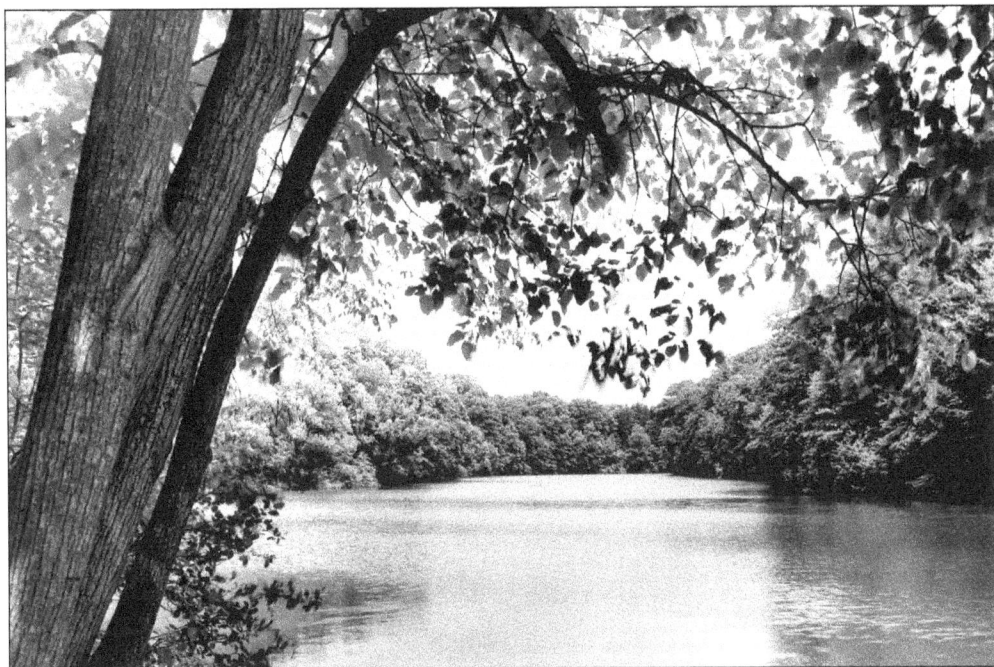

The pristine character of Lake Cohasset reflects Volney Rogers's belief that the beauty of nature should not be spoiled by commercialism or artificial decoration such as statuary or frivolous additions. (Courtesy of the *Vindicator*.)

Sediment had filled much of Lake Cohasset, and park commissioners decided to dredge it. In May 1949, the water level was lowered, allowing carp to be caught from the spillway.

MOONLIGHT ON THE NARROWS
MILLCREEK PARK
YOUNGSTOWN, OHIO

The Narrows, seen here, is the stretch of water between Lake Glacier Dam and the Mahoning River. The dam in the foreground is the 1904 Ice Dam built by the Youngstown Ice Company. Price Road winds in front of the houses.

Lake Glacier, Mill Creek Park, Youngstown, Ohio.

Lake Glacier is the park's second artificial lake, built in 1904–1905 and also part of Volney Rogers's plan for the park. The name derives from the glacial history of the area. The ancient Sangamon River, which flowed 300,000 years ago, emptied west of what one day would be Mill Creek. During the Ice Age, glacial materials advancing from the north filled up the Sangamon Valley and molded the topography of the area. Mill Creek later carved through the glacial deposits to create the Mill Creek Valley, where Lake Glacier sits.

Three men on the west shore observe the foam below Lake Glacier Dam on February 17, 1908. (Courtesy of the *Vindicator*.)

The Lake Glacier Dam is an E. Sherman Gould design. The concrete spillway, covered in sandstone, is 18 feet high and 160 feet wide. Price Road brought visitors into the park from Mahoning Avenue and carried traffic around the northern end of Lake Glacier and over Calvary Run. (Courtesy of the Mahoning Valley Historical Society.)

Alice Baldwin Lewis donated 70 acres and sold to the park additional acres to make possible the creation of Lake Newport, named for one of her Revolutionary War–era ancestors. The memorial rock with this information was placed originally at the Mary Newport Memorial Garden on the eastern side of the Lake Newport Dam. In 1954, the rock was moved to the newly relocated Newport Boat Landing. (Courtesy of the *Vindicator*.)

Following this large land acquisition in 1924, the park commissioners began construction of scenic drives and a large recreational lake. In this 1926 photograph, three workmen remove trees and grub out stumps in the Lake Newport basin. In the upper left, East Newport Drive is under construction.

46

This view, looking north, shows the location of the proposed Newport Dam. Here the topography begins to change from a broad meadow to a gorge with steeper hillsides.

The land was sculpted, and channels were cut to create several islands. Plants and flowers were rescued from the soon-to-be-flooded basin and replanted on the islands.

The Newport Dam (shown here) was constructed in 1928 using sandstone quarried in the park. Ralph L. Ingram was the park engineer, and Luther Fawcett, who designed the Lanterman's Falls Bridge in 1920, was the consulting engineer. Warren H. Manning was the landscape architect for the Newport Section. He and park superintendent Hugh Imlay, also a landscape architect, designed the drives and trails on the sides of the lake.

The Lake Newport Dam, constructed in 1928 to dam Mill Creek, created a 100-acre body of water. Lake Newport, stretching from the city of Youngstown into Boardman Township, is the largest and southernmost of the park's three major lakes and a popular location for fishing and sightseeing. (Courtesy of the *Vindicator*.)

The Newport Dam features observation decks on both sides. Here sightseers and a fisherman enjoy the view from the west side of the dam. The original, pre-1954 boat landing is visible in the background at the right, just above the decorative metal railing. (Courtesy of the *Vindicator*.)

Compare the designs of the Lake Newport and Lake Cohasset Dams. The Cohasset Dam, seen here, features a drop of several feet to a cascade made of straight, evenly placed stone steps. (Courtesy of the *Vindicator.*)

In this early-1960s photograph, visitors cruise on Lake Newport in the park's passenger boat. The Lake Newport Dam in the foreground, designed to create a cascading effect, was built with sandstone quarried in the park.

In August 1954, the Lake Newport Boat Landing was moved south to a new location on the western shore. Using part of an old millrace, park employees cut a winding channel for summer boat storage and landing. The channel also created a picnic island, seen at the right. (Courtesy of the *Vindicator*.)

The original location of the Newport Boat Landing was on the western shore, just south of the dam. Visitors could rent rowboats and canoes. The beginning of the West Newport Trail is visible in the lower right.

The new boat docks featured expanded parking and boat storage, a boat-launching ramp, and a picnic grove on an island reached by a footbridge. The park's maintenance crew moved the old caddy house from the golf course to this location for use as a rental office and refreshment stand.

Riding through the Mill Creek Gorge and its environs, Volney Rogers was inspired to save the area from impending development. Charles Eliot of Boston, the eminent landscape architect and partner of Frederick Law Olmsted, described the imposing Mill Creek Gorge to the park commissioners in an 1892 report: "Your gorge is one of the finest park scenes in America, and deserves most careful handling." (Courtesy of the *Vindicator*.)

What better way to spend a lazy August afternoon than to rent a boat at Lake Newport and drift out on the water? (Courtesy of the *Vindicator*.)

The Pump House Dam is located on Mill Creek, north of the Fording Bridge and south of Shields Road. The park dammed the creek here to create a small pond from which water was pumped to irrigate the golf course. This also was a spot suitable for a family outing, and for those able to jump the spillway, the dam provided a way to cross from East to West Golf Drive.

Bear Creek enters Mill Creek Park on the west side near McCollum and Bears Den Roads and flows east through Bears Den Ravine, the lower Bears Den Meadow, and Mirror Pond. It is one of Mill Creek's main tributaries. (Photograph © by Scott Lanz.)

Four

BRIDGES

The land bordering Mill Creek in the original 400 acres of the park contained many tributaries and deep side ravines. This topography necessitated the construction of several bridges to accommodate vehicles and foot traffic on the planned drives and trails. In 1891, when the park was founded, people could cross Mill Creek at only a few places: the High Bridge on the Canfield Road at Lanterman's Falls, Old Furnace Road Bridge at Pioneer Pavilion, and the Mahoning Avenue Bridge, where Mill Creek entered the Mahoning River. The first park bridge to span Mill Creek was the Slippery Rock Bridge, built in 1895. Several stone bridges, including the magnificent 1913 Parapet Bridge, were later constructed to accommodate automobiles, which had begun to replace the horse-and-buggy traffic of the park's first two decades. These stone spans used materials quarried in or near the park and were designed by architects such as Julius Schweinfurth and the Boston firm of Shepley Rutan and Coolidge. Wooden bridges were built for the small tributaries and trails.

Volney Rogers used bridge design to help define the unique character of the park, creating spans as architectural gateways to a new land.

Axe Factory Run Bridge spans a tributary of Mill Creek on the west side of Lake Cohasset. The run was named for John Ross's axe factory, which operated nearby in the 1830s.

An old covered bridge on Truesdale Road in Boardman Township provided passage over Mill Creek at the south end of what is now Lake Newport. This section of the old Truesdale Road is now underwater.

Visitors trekking to the popular Sulphur Spring in the Mill Creek Gorge used this footbridge, which connected Valley Drive with the trail to the popular destination. Above the sign marked "Main Ramble" is a warning of a $10 fine for cutting or injuring any park tree, shrub, seat, or bridge.

The Axe Factory Run Bridge was built of stone in 1913.

The High Bridge spanning Mill Creek Gorge was constructed in the 1880s. Passersby on Canfield Road were afforded a magnificent view of Lanterman's Falls and Mill.

The Orchard Meadow Bridge over Bear Creek was built in 1895. This photograph, taken in December 1903, shows Orchard Meadow in the foreground and the Tanner Homestead in the background.

Seen here in flood stage, Bear Creek rushes under Orchard Meadow Bridge on its course to join Mill Creek. Bear Creek originates in the north Raccoon Road and Norquest Boulevard section of Austintown. (Courtesy of the *Vindicator*.)

The Suspension Bridge, which spans Mill Creek and connects the east and west sides of the park, was erected in 1895. Following the wishes of Volney Rogers to create a fanciful park entrance, Charles Fowler of the Youngstown Bridge Company designed the structure. The oldest bridge in Mill Creek Park, it is 86 feet long and 32 feet wide.

Over the years, the Suspension Bridge has been known by many names, including the White Bridge, Silver Bridge, Fairy Tale Bridge, Castle Bridge, and Cinderella Bridge. This postcard dates from January 1912.

The Parapet Bridge on the east side of Lake Glacier was constructed in 1913. Using sketches by park superintendent Bruce Rogers, architect and landscape designer Julius Schweinfurth created a striking masterpiece with massive upright boulders and a graceful arch. From the four viewing platforms, visitors could look east to Spring Brook Ravine and west to Lake Glacier.

The longest of the park's stone arch structures, the Parapet Bridge continues to be the most photographed span in Mill Creek Park. The irregular stone parapets decorating the top of the span have given rise to other more descriptive names, such as the Dragon Bridge and the Prehistoric Bridge.

A family picnic on the banks of Cascade Run is framed by Cascade Run Bridge, built in 1913.
(Courtesy of the *Vindicator*.)

The original Slippery Rock Bridge, constructed of steel with sandstone abutments, crossed Mill Creek south of present-day Lake Glacier. It was razed in 1958 to make way for a wider span. (Courtesy of the Mahoning Valley Historical Society.)

Funds from a 1954 park levy allowed the start of construction on a wider Slippery Rock Bridge in 1958. Engineered by Robert Schomer, the new bridge was dedicated on September 30, 1959.

Young fishermen enjoy a summer afternoon on Slippery Rock Bridge in 1950. Notice the design elements of the steel bridge railing and compare them to similar elements in the Suspension Bridge on page 59.

Constructed in 1913, the same year as Axe Factory Run Bridge, the Cascade Run Bridge carries Valley Drive over this tributary of Mill Creek.

The Lanterman's Falls Bridge, a concrete span, was built in 1920 to replace the old High Bridge. Hired by Mill Creek Park in 1919 as a consultant, Luther Fawcett served as engineer for the new bridge, which today carries Route 62 across Mill Creek Gorge.

The Japanese Bridge, built in 1958, is an arched footbridge crossing Calvary Run. To the east in the background is Lake Glacier. The light pole for the lake's skating area is visible in the right background. (Courtesy of the *Vindicator*.)

Five

VISTAS

The design of the landscape and placement of drives and trails were calculated to provide superior vantage points for viewing the scenic beauty of Mill Creek Park. Benches positioned at strategic spots along the trails allowed visitors to contemplate the views in leisurely fashion. Volney Rogers personally marked certain trees to be cut down to create vistas that would suddenly surprise and delight the park visitor. Though aware of the need for immediate improvements, he had the vision and patience for long-range planning. Park commissioner Charles Robinson explained, "Mr. Rogers always looked forward. . . . He could see how the thing would look when it was completed. To him ten or twenty years were no more than a week or two." For example, the East Cohasset Ramble, which borders Lake Cohasset, was created six years before the lake itself. This was possible because Rogers could see the lake in his mind long before it became a reality.

Rogers also had the wisdom to consult nationally prominent experts in landscape architecture, such as Charles Eliot and H. W. S. Cleveland. In the 1920s, when the park quintupled in size, Warren H. Manning played a key role in shaping the land, especially in the Lake Newport area. Although the means by which a person travels in the park have evolved from horse and buggy to streetcar to automobile, a visitor's appreciation of the scenic vistas remains unchanged.

The Lake Glacier overlook is a romantic vista looking south from Fellows Riverside Gardens.

The inviting stone steps on the west side of Mill Creek and the Suspension Bridge lead to an area of massive boulders, small caves, and defunct coal mines. From there, a footpath connects to the Cascade Ravine Trail. One of the caves—Witch's Cave—was a daring place for the young to visit. It was eventually bricked up and sealed for safety reasons.

This photograph was taken from the east bank of the Mill Creek Narrows. The Lake Glacier Dam appears in the center, and Price Road curves around the right bank. Lake Glacier is the park's second and most northern lake.

The Mill Creek Golf Course was designed in 1928 by famed golf course architect Donald Ross. Nestled in the beauty and splendor of a park setting, the course offers playing experiences that test all levels of players. The stately landscape with magnificent deciduous and evergreen trees and meandering streams makes this one of Ohio's prettiest public courses.

The arching tree near Slippery Rock frames the way for a day's adventure in the park.

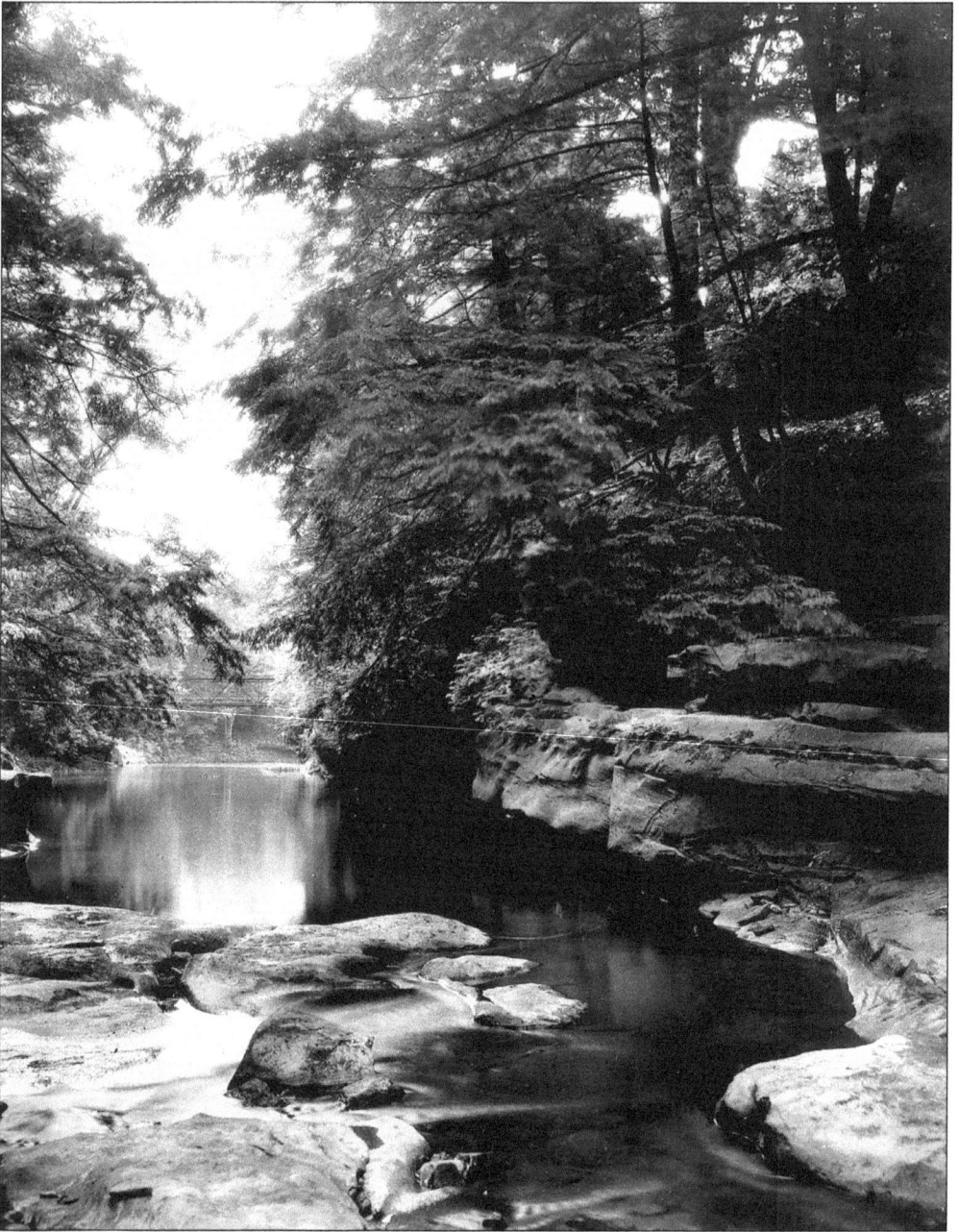

Professional photographer Walter Bartz was employed by Youngstown Sheet and Tube, where park commissioner Charles Robinson was a top executive. Bartz spent much time photographing and filming beautiful spots in the park. Here he has captured the mystery of the Pool of Shadows above Lanterman's Falls. In August 1921, renowned designer Warren H. Manning told the *Vindicator*, "The people of Youngstown cannot appreciate what they have in Youngstown. Hardly any park in the country has anything to compare with it." Manning said that this was particularly true of the magnificent scenery shown here around Lanterman's Falls.

On August 6, 1941, the 50th anniversary of the park was celebrated with a tree planting in honor of the first superintendent, Bruce Rogers, who served from 1891 to 1918. In this photograph, park policeman Bill Klingensmith holds the shovel. The species selected was a cucumber tree, *magnolia acuminate*, one of the largest and most resilient magnolias. An excellent shade tree, it is named for its green, unripe fruit, which resembles a small cucumber.

The Rock Ridge Recreation Area is under development in 1954. Warren H. Manning had advocated the park's acquisition of this large field for playgrounds and recreation in 1921. The intersection of Belle Vista Avenue and McCollum Road, the site's entrance, appears on the left. Newly planted crab apple and pine trees are sprinkled along the McCollum Road side of the parcel, where the Par 3 Golf Course would be built in 1962. The larger of the two rectangular pads is the parking lot. The smaller pad to the right is the foundation for the basketball, tennis, and shuffleboard courts. The land on the upper right was used for an archery range.

The Edith Kauffman Memorial Quarry Garden was built on the site of a late-19th-century quarry. The abandoned quarry along Glenwood Avenue near Mill Creek Park had become an eyesore. Edith Kauffman, president of the Garden Club of Youngstown, persuaded property owners to donate land to the park for the development of a garden. After the land was deeded to the park in 1928, the garden was designed to be a secluded sanctuary for people as well as birds. Birdhouses and birdbaths were installed. In recognition of Edith Kauffman's efforts, the garden was named in her honor in 1933. (Courtesy of the *Vindicator*.)

Lake Newport, created in 1928, is the third and largest lake in the park. Seen through three stately birch trees, the quiet beauty of the 100-acre lake is a well-known remedy for the urban blues. (Courtesy of the *Vindicator*.)

An old millrace at Lake Newport was dredged to form a picnic island that opened in August 1954. A steel footbridge carried happy picnickers to the new site. The island was named for park commissioner Robert K. Smythe in 1957, following his death. (Courtesy of the *Vindicator*.)

In 1932, the Garden Club of Youngstown purchased 8,000 bulbs to plant on the east side of Lake Newport as part of a beautification plan for the Newport Section of the park. Every spring, visitors flock to Daffodil Meadow to take in the early show of color. Landscape architect Warren H. Manning believed that park design should adapt to accommodate people's views from automobiles. Because visitors were traveling at faster speeds, he specified that vistas should appear at the end of vision lines as people were driving toward them rather than on the sides of roads, which would be quickly passed. Flowers were to be planted in masses in order to catch the eye. (Courtesy of the *Vindicator.*)

The solitude of a fall afternoon in October 1967 fills the air over Lake Newport. (Courtesy of the *Vindicator.*)

The Lake Glacier Boathouse offers pedal boat and rowboat rentals and a boat launch. Shown here in October 1969, the passenger boat glides beyond the Japanese Bridge. This bridge over Calvary Run is a favorite spot for bridal party photographs. (Courtesy of the *Vindicator*.)

Cascade Run, which enters the park on the west side, has carved a ravine into the layers of stone on its way to Lake Cohasset.

The South Terrace at Fellows Riverside Gardens overlooks one of the park's most spectacular vistas. On this high bluff over Price Road and the Old Log Cabin, many marriages have been proposed. The contrast between this southern look over the peaceful Mill Creek Valley and the North Terrace, with its view of urban Youngstown, echoes the difference that Volney Rogers sensed between the industrialized Mahoning Valley and the quiet environs of Mill Creek. Here it is easiest to see what his heart, mind, and desire brought to fruition. (Courtesy of the *Vindicator*.)

Six

STRUCTURES AND ATTRACTIONS

Following approval of the park plan by Youngstown voters in 1891, the newly appointed commissioners—Volney Rogers, Henry Tod, and Robert Mackey—immediately recognized the need to build facilities that would encourage visitors to spend time in the park. Their first project was to remodel Pioneer Pavilion into a rental facility for social gatherings. In 1910, Julius Schweinfurth was hired to design a new open-air pavilion in the Slippery Rock area. At first called the New Pavilion to distinguish it from Pioneer Pavilion, this rustic structure, which could hold 150 guests, soon became known as Slippery Rock Pavilion. In the 1920s, the park added Chestnut Hill Pavilion, a golf course designed by Donald Ross, and several comfort stations. In the 1930s, Birch Hill Cabin, Bears Den Cabin, and Stitt Pavilion were added, and the park converted German Lanterman's old gristmill to the Old Mill Museum.

The Old Log Cabin is another example of a historic structure whose origins predate the founding of Mill Creek Park.

The Old Log Cabin, built about 1814, is nestled in the hillside on the north shore of Lake Glacier. Originally located in the Rock Ridge area, it was moved to the present location around the time of the Civil War. Youngstown physician Dr. Timothy Woodbridge owned the cabin and used it as a medical office. The park purchased the property in 1892. First used as an employee residence, the cabin was remodeled in 1934 as a rental facility for parties and gatherings. The Old Log Cabin is one of the oldest buildings in Mahoning County.

Crowds came daily to the Sulphur Spring to fill jugs with water. Volney Rogers stated in the July 23, 1900, *Vindicator*, "I am glad there are so many persons visiting this place. We intend to fix the springs up as soon as possible." Improvements included the seating shown in this postcard. The August 8, 1900, *Vindicator* reported, "The crowd of yesterday contained many new faces, and the old timers were also there in larger numbers than even before. The water has worked such a world of good to so many people, that they cannot stay away, and they recommend the water cure to all of their friends for anything from an ingrowing toe nail to a broken leg."

This postcard of the charming Pioneer Pavilion and its environs illustrates the facility's status as a scenic icon. This vista was popularized in a long series of postcards. The original Old Furnace Bridge is pictured on the right.

The fully restored Lanterman's Mill and replica covered bridge continue as an important community icon today, just as in the 1880s. Thanks to a caring and generous $600,000 grant from the Beecher family, the mill operates again as it did in the past, grinding grain and serving as a reminder of the area's pioneer heritage. Eleanor Beecher Flad, great-granddaughter of German Lanterman, and her children have taken an active role in preserving the legacy left to the valley by Volney Rogers. C. Robert Buchanan and Associates were hired for the complicated mill restoration project. Robert J. Schomer, park engineer, served as project engineer for the mill's renovation. The new covered bridge, built in 1989, was designed by Schomer, who styled it after the original—open on all sides to allow viewing of the natural beauty up- and downstream. As the original stone abutments were still visible, Schomer sited his plan at the same spot. The new span is a critical connector for the park's trail system, as well as a route to the mill for emergency vehicles, offering universal access. Lanterman's Mill has emerged from the restoration as a park landmark, alive with visitors, and integral to the park's nature and history programs.

Slippery Rock Pavilion, built in 1910–1911, became the park's first open-air pavilion. Architect Julius Schweinfurth used massive supports of native sandstone and a tile roof to create a distinctive design. The name reflects a local legend of a boy swimming at Mill Creek who slipped off a large rock and drowned.

Seating 150 people, Slippery Rock Pavilion is a popular location for family reunions, church outings, and group gatherings. A children's playground and a foot trail are adjacent to the structure.

The park's most popular site for large group picnics is Slippery Rock Pavilion. This photograph likely dates from the early 1950s. Note the individual Isaly Dairy Company glass milk bottles and the china place settings; the picnic clearly was held before paper plates and cups became common.

The project underway in March 1922 was the "Big Cut"—the construction of the West Drive. The park's consulting landscape architect from 1920 to 1929 was Warren H. Manning, who had worked for Frederick Law Olmsted for eight years before starting his own firm and was close to fellow designer Charles Eliot, who had worked on designing earlier sections of the park with Volney Rogers.

The retaining wall, now called the Wall Garden, was finished with stone blocks from Bears Den Quarry and a variety of rock garden plants, primarily basket-of-gold and creeping phlox. This work was done to stabilize the hillside on West Drive. Located under Lookout Point, the retaining wall is 552 feet long and 54 feet wide.

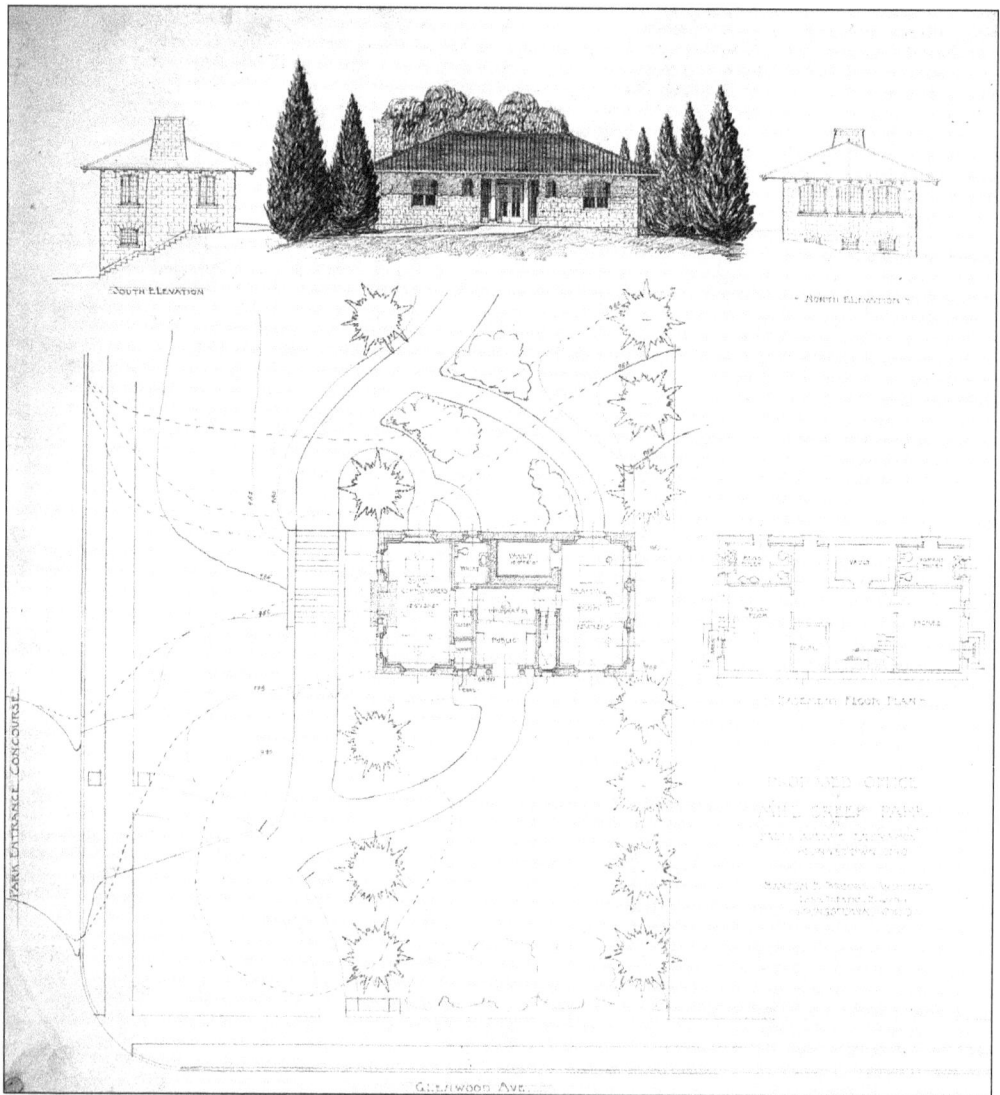

Shown here is the preliminary sketch of the administration building designed by Barton E. Brooke in August 1921. The building was constructed in 1922 at the corner of Glenwood and Falls Avenues on the former site of Bruce Rogers's home. Brooke and his partner, Harold R. Dyer, designed many grand homes near the park on Volney Road and Ottawa and Genesee Drives.

The completed park administration building at 816 Glenwood Avenue, shown here in June 1923, features large columns and sandstone construction. The stone carving on the lintel reads "Mill Creek."

Park police standing in front of the entrance to the administration building in 1931 include, from left to right, John Kofler, J. F. Douglass, Mert Boyle, Walter Scholl, Michael King, Edwin Baehler, and superintendent Al Davies. The squad was responsible for patrolling the parklands between Mahoning Avenue and Boardman-Canfield Road. During the summer, the patrol increased to 10 officers. Walter Scholl policed on horseback from 1928 until his promotion to recreation director in 1941. Retiring in 1972, Scholl served for 44 years, the longest career in park history. As a boy, Al Davies worked various jobs for the park: locker boy, boatman, and lifeguard. Following his graduation from Ohio Wesleyan University, he taught physical education in the Boardman schools. His adult tenure at the park began when he was hired as recreation director and police captain by superintendent Hugh Imlay in 1927. He was appointed superintendent in 1936 and served until 1967. (Courtesy of the *Vindicator*.)

Boston architect Barton E. Brooke moved to Youngstown to design employee housing for Youngstown Sheet and Tube. In 1922, he planned the one-story restroom addition to Pioneer Pavilion, shown to the left.

Barton E. Brooke also planned the golf course fieldhouse in 1929. The design featured a stone exterior and held a dining room, locker rooms, and lounging areas. Due to budget constraints, the exterior façade was changed to stucco.

Chestnut Hill Pavilion, shown being built in June 1923, is another Barton E. Brooke design. The name of the picnic structure draws from a stand of magnificent chestnut trees that once stood in this section. The pavilion, located on Chestnut Hill Drive near Bears Den Road, features an open fireplace, a large meadow area, and a children's playground.

Bears Den Drive, on the left, and the Cross Drive, on the right, are shown here under construction. The curbing being installed is made of stone. The development in the Bears Den area began after the property was purchased in 1921. The land contained remnants of early quarries, as well as massive sandstone boulders that have been climbed over and picnicked on for generations.

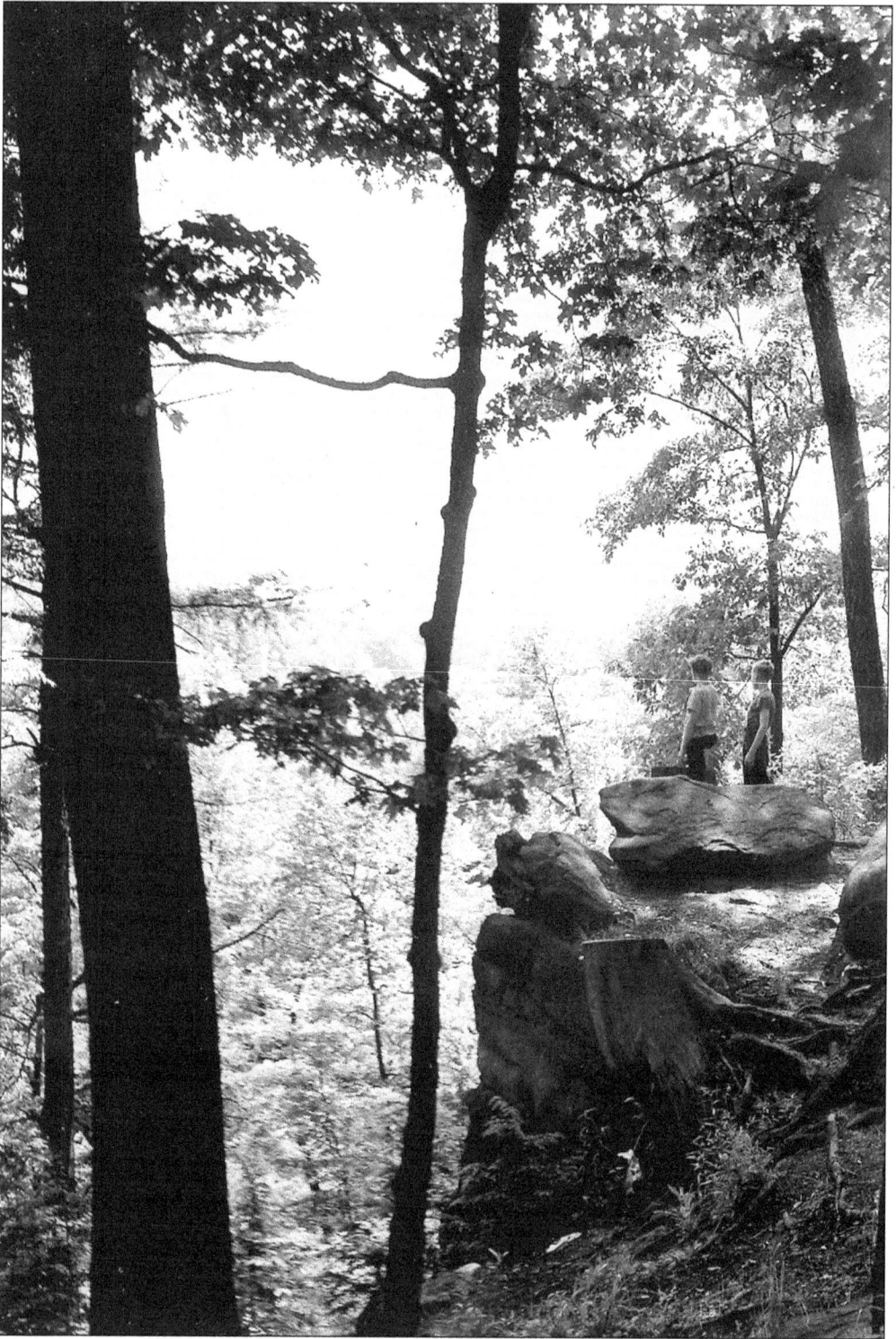

Two boys look out above the East Gorge Trail from a vantage point near the Old Mill parking lot in 1945. (Courtesy of the *Vindicator*.)

In 1945, park visitors take in the scenery on the drive from the Fresh Air Camp to the Lily Pond. (Courtesy of the *Vindicator*.)

The Charles Robinson home, located at 840 Old Furnace Road, was designed by architect Charles F. Owsley in 1912. A good friend of Volney Rogers, Robinson served as park commissioner from 1920 to 1945. To connect the nearby Edith Kauffman Quarry Garden to the Slippery Rock area, the Robinsons donated a parcel containing a lush, wooded ravine. Mrs. Robinson gave more land in 1947 in memory of her husband. In 1951, Judge John W. Ford purchased the residence. The judge's children gifted the property to the park in 1968.

The Junior League of Youngstown aided in the conversion of the former Judge Ford residence to a nature education center. When the park ran short of funds, the league's environmental action committee, headed by Barbara McCrudden, arranged for a grant of $5,000. Shown at the Ford Nature Education Center, from left to right, are Mary Ann Brenner, Judy Hoover, Lynn Doyle, park superintendent Charles Wedekind, and commissioner K. Calvin Sommer. The center opened in June 1972 as the home of the park's nature education program. (Courtesy of the *Vindicator*.)

Rustic wooden guardrails, used at many places in the park, line the trail leading to the east side of the Newport Dam. (Courtesy of the *Vindicator*.)

Virginia Axtmann, proponent of a nature trail with universal access for the disabled, was also responsible for obtaining a substantial portion of the funds necessary for the project. Other fund-raising efforts were led by the Youngstown Society for the Blind and Disabled and the Youngstown Hospital Association employees, who sold surgical scrub suits to raise money for the $8,000 nature trail. Taking part in the groundbreaking on August 3, 1981, from left to right, are park commissioner Avetis Darvanan, Easter Seals director Andrew Douglas, Joey Poschner, park commissioner Ken McMahon, and Virginia Axtmann. Located adjacent to the Ford Nature Center, the first portion of the trail was completed in 1982, and in 1990, the extended trail was finished and named the Virginia J. Axtmann Nature Trail for All People. (Courtesy of the *Vindicator*.)

In May 1985, the Colonial Dames of the XVII Century, Stephen Hopkins Chapter of Warren, dedicated a plaque over the fireplace at the Old Log Cabin. Evidence suggests that chapter member Barbara McKinney Kroehle's great-great-grandparents Mr. and Mrs. Camden Cleveland built the cabin about 1814. (Courtesy of the *Vindicator*.)

General foreman Mark Nesbitt keeps the Old Log Cabin, one of the county's oldest surviving structures, in good shape, ready for its next rental. (Courtesy of the *Vindicator*.)

Seven

RECREATION

Volney Rogers and subsequent park planners laid out specific areas for a multitude of recreation activities. Rogers described his philosophy on recreation best in his 1904 book *A Partial Description of Mill Creek Park*: "Every city should have numerous open spaces distributed throughout its area, and particularly in thickly populated districts; so that there may be a convenient oasis, or green place for pure air, bright sunshine, and grateful shade for daily rest and recreation for all. In addition to this there should be public playgrounds for children in the charge of a keeper, who would enforce good morals and proper behavior."

Mill Creek Park provides the unique mix of both passive and active recreation facilities. Visitors can take advantage of picnic grounds and pavilions, 15 miles of hiking trails, 20 miles of scenic drives, a 36-hole Donald Ross–designed golf course, an 18-hole par 3 golf course, numerous playgrounds, tennis, basketball, and volleyball courts, lighted sledding hills, cross-country ski courses, boating centers, lake fishing, and a variety of ballfields.

The 1950 Volney Rogers Football League Champions, wearing assorted styles of leather headgear, pose for the record books with recreation director Walter "Farmer" Scholl. Scholl fostered many youth athletic programs at Volney Rogers Field during his 31-year tenure in recreation. By 1963, there were 17 football teams with over 500 players in the league.

A costumed young lady with ballet slippers gracefully poses for the camera at Volney Rogers Playground in 1923.

Young girls in petal dresses take part in a competition at Volney Rogers Playground in 1923.

E. W. Vickers, the park's first naturalist, leads a group hike through Cascade Ravine. Vickers is credited with planting the Wall Garden and initiating both the Old Mill Museum and the park's nature education programming. In 1930, he organized a group of 18 men to rescue 40,000 wildflowers, including 25,000 bluebells, from the land about to be flooded for the Meander Reservoir. The wildflowers were planted throughout the 1,300 acres of the park.

After a long, hard hike through the rugged Mill Creek Gorge, E. W. Vickers stands in the foreground with his walking stick. Directly behind him in the cap is his son, assistant naturalist Lindley. For this father-and-son team, their love of nature was both vocation and avocation. The man to the right of Lindley is Al Davies, park superintendent.

This ceremony under the picnic pavilion was part of the 1923 Volney Rogers Playground Carnival Days. The extensive summer programming included popular activities and contests.

Children experience views of the park from the diving platform at Lake Glacier, located near the present-day Lake Glacier Boathouse. Swimming was a significant recreational activity at Lakes Glacier and Cohasset until the late 1920s, when contamination from Youngstown's sewers made the waters unfit for this sport.

Prior to recreation director Walter Scholl's introduction of baseball and football leagues to Volney Rogers Field, the program focused primarily on softball. This photograph celebrates the Rogers Seniors Softball Champions of 1940. Volney Rogers Field and Playground was the first recreational area developed by the park. The 18-acre recreational complex, located between Glenwood Avenue and East Glacier Drive, was built in 1921. Landscape architect Hugh Imlay was park superintendent during the design and construction of the facility.

After acquiring in 1935 the former grounds of the Mill Creek Riding Club for $15,000, the park converted the area into an archery range. Thanks to Olympic archery events in 1900, 1904, 1908, and 1920 for men and 1904 and 1908 for women, archery became an immensely popular sport nationwide for several decades. The range area of the park was later developed into the 10-acre Kirkmere Recreation Area, which opened in 1956. In 1988, this facility was named for Walter H. Scholl, recreation director for 31 years. This was the first time a facility was named for a park employee.

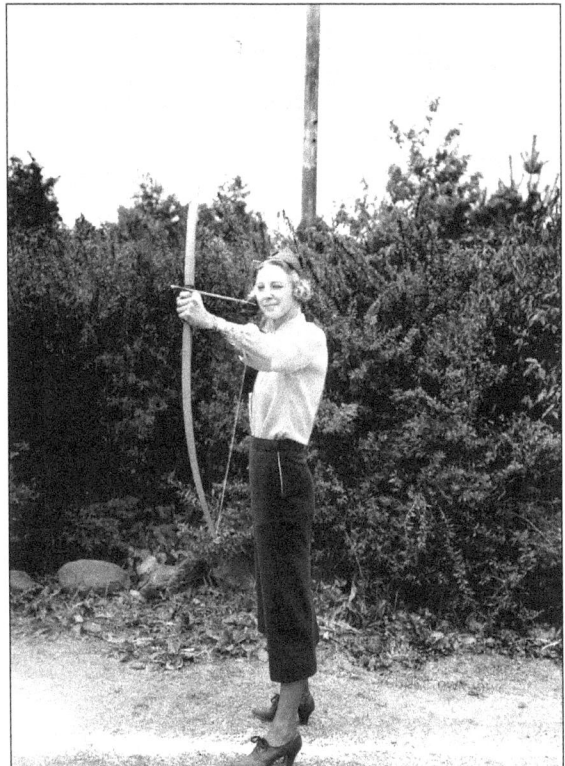

Archery clubs and competitions flourished in Mill Creek Park, and women as well as men took advantage of the park's archery range.

97

A very young player at the Volney Rogers Field tennis courts balances his racquet with style.

The seven tennis courts at Volney Rogers Field have for decades been the site of local tournaments, high school matches, and public play. Superior clay construction yielded a championship-level facility, and lights for evening matches added to the sophistication of the complex.

Youngstown artist and professional photographer Charles Hoover sketches Lanterman's Mill in October 1939 at the age of 74. Hoover created his first view of the mill when he was 13, going on to paint the mill over a thousand times, in all seasons. He taught landscape painting for private classes in Mill Creek Park from 1918 to 1921.

Girl Scouts from Chaney High School honor Volney Rogers and the 50th anniversary of Mill Creek Park with a tree planting along East Newport Drive in the children's planting area. Every child who attended this April 1941 ceremony received a sapling to plant. Scout troops, garden clubs, and other civic groups have supported the park with countless hours of volunteer work.

From the vantage point of East Cohasset Drive, a photographer captures a fresh snow and a group of eager skiers at Ski Hill. Popular in the 1930s and 1940s, Ski Hill was extensively used for skiing, sledding, and tobogganing. After several serious accidents, the hill was closed in the early 1980s.

Lake Newport is the site of a high school hockey tournament in January 1940.

Ice-skating on Lake Newport was a popular winter activity for decades. In the evening, bonfires provided warmth, light, and a chance for social interaction. This photograph was taken in 1941.

Prizes were awarded in these categories in the 1945 Doll Show at Volney Rogers Playground: Prettiest Doll, Largest Doll, Smallest Doll, Largest Number Entered, Best Dressed Doll, and Best Baby Carriage.

During the summer, children flocked to the park and Volney Rogers Field for a variety of activities, crafts, and contests. The appreciation for horticulture was considered a highly desirable trait in children, as well as adults. This flower show photograph was taken in 1946.

This three-legged race was an event in the Inter-Playground Track Meet held in August 1944. Besides plenty of room for track-and-field events, Volney Rogers Field offered tennis and basketball courts, baseball diamonds, football fields, a playground, and a shelter house. In the field's early years, recreation director Walter Scholl, also known as Farmer Scholl, groomed the grounds using a Model T Ford and a set of bedsprings.

From "onesies" to "tensies," the popular childhood game of jacks was a classic summer competition at Volney Rogers Playground. Dorothy Wallis, the 1940 Jacks Champion, shows off her skills.

Volney Rogers Playground Carnival Days attracted hundreds of kids and their families for fun and competition. Youth from diverse backgrounds shared this park backdrop for a multitude of summer memories.

The open spaces of Mill Creek Park have been used on many occasions to gather sizable groups for theater presentations and historic reenactments. To commemorate Mill Creek Park's 50th anniversary in April 1941, a Chaney High School class presented a dramatic scene depicting the life's work of Volney Rogers. Chaney seniors Paul Herman and William Hura wrote and directed the play, Michael Kirwan Jr. portrayed Volney Rogers, and Eric Reinthaler played a *Vindicator* reporter interviewing him.

A boy's favorite 1940s pastime—fishing from the banks of Lake Newport—sometimes left too little time for chores and studying. Many mothers had to come to the park to retrieve their children for meals and sleep.

Promising track stars practice at the Slippery Rock Meadow in the 1950s. The racer on the left sports a Boardman Spartans T-shirt.

Park naturalist Lindley Vickers raises his hat to the photographer on a hike through Bears Den Ravine in 1949. During his tenure from 1947 to 1970, Vickers guided 500,000 children on nature walks, personally walking 32,000 miles.

Lindley Vickers sits at his desk in the Old Mill Museum at Lanterman's Falls in March 1951. A portrait of Volney Rogers hangs on the wall. (Courtesy of the *Vindicator*.)

The Rock Ridge Recreation Area, located on the west side of Youngstown, opened in 1956. The park purchased the 65-acre tract from the federal government in 1947. Carl Rust Parker, a consultant with Olmsted Brothers of Brookline, Massachusetts, recommended active recreational uses for the area. Development of the new recreation area took over eight years at a cost of more than $200,000 and followed the passage of a 1954 park levy. Facilities in 1958 included a children's playground with slides, swings, and a spray pool; picnic areas; fields for baseball and football; tennis, basketball, horseshoe, and shuffleboard courts; a coasting (sledding) hill; and an archery range. The complex was renamed to honor James L. Wick Jr., recently retired park commissioner, in September 1958. (Courtesy of the *Vindicator*.)

Lake Newport provides the setting for a calm, lazy day, complete with a kitchen chair. (Courtesy of the *Vindicator*.)

Volney Rogers wrote the following in 1904: "Play with the children; teach them the names and uses of Nature's gifts about them; point them to the trees, birds, herbage and flowers, tell them the name and habits of each, and you will have sown the seeds for something ennobling in their hearts that will never be forgotten." (Courtesy of the *Vindicator*.)

The *Glacier*, a whimsical passenger boat, offered pleasure rides on Lake Glacier, often with a park naturalist aboard.

There was no better spot to find peace and relaxation in the summer of 1945 than on the banks of Lake Newport. (Courtesy of the *Vindicator*.)

Two boys admire a splendid vista in the northern section of Mill Creek Park in 1945. (Courtesy of the *Vindicator*.)

In the 1920s, Mill Creek Park hired Scottish-born Donald Ross, the father of American golf course architecture, to design a 36-hole course between Route 224 and Shields Road in Boardman Township. Pictured here is the excavation of the No. 1 tee on the North Course using horse-drawn implements. The first 18 holes opened in 1928, the next 9 in 1932, and the last 9 in 1937. In 1998, *Golfweek* selected the South Course as one of America's 30 Best Municipal Courses.

Sunday golfers begin their round at the No. 1 tee on the North Course in July 1954. The golf course has been home to countless summer leagues with thousands of rounds of weekly play.

The golf course fieldhouse, designed by Barton E. Brooke and Harold Dyer, was constructed in 1929. Educated in Boston, Brooke moved to Youngstown in 1917. He and Dyer also designed the clubhouse at the Youngstown Country Club.

Wanda Maxim, Anne Metzinger, and Alice Mayo (from left to right) enjoy a November bike ride near the Slippery Rock Pavilion in 1966. (Courtesy of the *Vindicator*.)

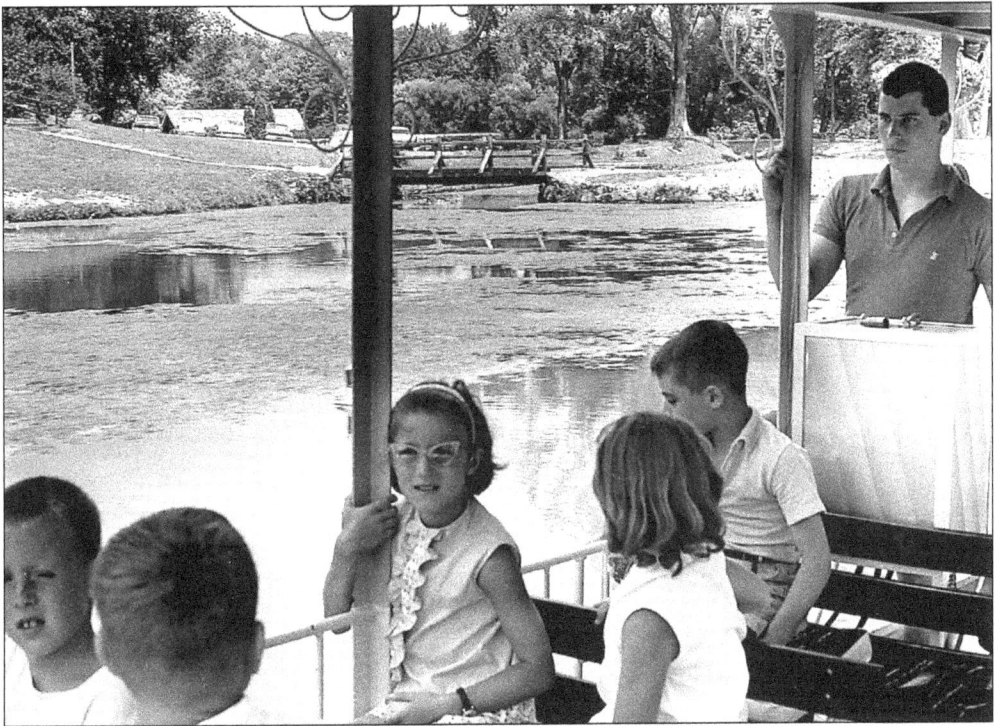

Tom Crago pilots the Lake Newport passenger boat north of Smythe Island in 1961.

The *Glacier* passenger boat cruises Lake Glacier. The waterwheels are purely decorative on this pontoon boat.

Shoreline fishing around Lakes Glacier and Newport was not permitted until July 1, when the banks would be drier and the nesting season over. These boys enjoy fishing from boats on Lake Newport in May 1962. (Courtesy of the *Vindicator*.)

To promote a 1984 levy, park naturalist Bill Whitehouse (left), recreation director Tom Bresko, and mascot Captain Parker (Flora Doraski, assistant naturalist) remind the public that the park depends on taxpayers' support for capital funds. (Courtesy of the *Vindicator*.)

Naturalist Megan Jones presents a program at the Ford Nature and Education Center. Since the Ford Center opening in 1972, hundreds of school classes from all parts of Mahoning, Trumbull, and Columbiana Counties have benefitted from the park's nature education programming. (Courtesy of the *Vindicator*.)

Bill Whitehouse (right) lectures to Dr. Clyde Vanaman's Youngstown State University graduate education class on the back lawn of the Ford Nature and Education Center. (Courtesy of the *Vindicator*.)

Eight

FELLOWS RIVERSIDE GARDENS

Elizabeth Fellows's dream of a garden for all to come and enjoy, free of charge, perpetuates the legacy of park founder Volney Rogers by providing another green backdrop for family memories while preserving the open space for generations to come. Like Mill Creek Park itself, Fellows Riverside Gardens is designed to serve the educational and recreational needs of the general public in a scenic and healthful environment.

Fellows Riverside Gardens features a rolling landscape of remarkable beauty. Since the first planting in 1963, gardeners and plant lovers have been mesmerized by the diverse collections throughout its 12 acres. Roses of all classes are displayed, along with specialty collections of shade, herb, and rock garden plants. The scenic vistas, labeled trees and shrubs, and colorful seasonal displays of annuals, perennials, and flowering bulbs have drawn millions of visitors from around the world to the lands on the bluff overlooking Lake Glacier.

The graceful Victorian Gazebo stands beyond the Sommer Fountain. The fountain was dedicated in May 1977 to honor the president of the board of park commissioners, K. Calvin Sommer. Designed by Howard Schafer of C. Robert Buchanan and Associates and built by the Aberdeen Company, the improvement cost about $38,000.

Elizabeth Rudge Fellows (1861–1958) and Samuel Fellows (1856–1942) grew up in Youngstown, attended the Rayen School, and married in 1883. Samuel pursued a successful career in the iron and steel industry. Elizabeth developed a love of gardening, specializing in perennials and roses. In 1931, they retired to family-owned lands on Mahoning Avenue overlooking Mill Creek Park. As Samuel and Elizabeth were childless, Samuel directed in his will that Elizabeth leave their property to charity. Shortly after his death, Elizabeth visited park superintendent Al Davies. Impressed by her tour, she changed her will one month after Samuel's death, stipulating that her lands be given to the park. Elizabeth also provided an endowment fund to support the costs of construction and operation of a large public garden. At the age of 96, she died at home from pneumonia on March 19, 1958. At the March 25 park board meeting, the commissioners agreed to accept Elizabeth Fellows's magnificent tribute in memory of Samuel's parents, Benjamin and Mary Fellows.

John L. Paolano was hired to design Fellows Riverside Gardens. An earlier plan by Olmsted Brothers in 1960 had been rejected as too costly and formal. Born in Italy in 1902, Paolano graduated from The Ohio State University and began a distinguished career in landscape architecture. In addition to his private practice, he worked for the National Park Service in Washington, D.C., on Potomac projects, including the Tidal Basin. Paolano's philosophy of landscape design for everyone, not just the upper crust, mirrored the wishes of Elizabeth Fellows's will to create "a beauty spot to be enjoyed by all, and particularly the poor." (Courtesy of the *Akron Beacon Journal*.)

Paolano's design for the gardens retained the existing stand of trees and emphasized the rolling topography of the property. This photograph dates from September 1965, prior to the installation of a fountain and gazebo. The public display garden was developed to include a wide range of landscape plants appropriate to northeast Ohio. Specimens were selected to give four seasons of interest, color, and texture. (© 2005, Mary Hoerner.)

Landscape architect John L. Paolano inspects the installation of the new gardens and the construction of the South Terrace in September 1965. His design embraced Elizabeth Fellows's wish for a blending of beauty and nature rather than a more formal installation. The two flagstone terraces, one overlooking Lake Glacier, a planned design feature, and the other, perched over the random and sprawling urban industrialized valley, give visitors a startling lesson in the contrasting landscapes. (© 2005, Mary Hoerner.)

In the distance, Paolano views the rose allée. He used an Italian design with poles and chains and planted 50 species of climbing roses to create walls of flowers. Later, in other areas of the gardens, roses of all classes—from shrub to botanical to hybrid perpetual—would be planted. (© 2005, Mary Hoerner.)

In 1964, park staff work in the modern rose garden as members of the Garden Forum of Greater Youngstown look on. Note the young boxwood and Japanese yews that will form hedges to enclose this garden. The modern rose garden was the first garden area to be constructed and planted, beginning in 1963. (Courtesy of the *Vindicator*.)

Andrew Knauer, the park's first horticulturist, inspects the new sign at the North Terrace overlooking downtown Youngstown. (Courtesy of the *Vindicator*.)

Dedication of the Garden Center on June 13, 1964, fulfilled a 30-year dream for the Garden Forum of Greater Youngstown. Owned and improved by Mill Creek Park, the center was presented to Garden Forum president Mrs. James L. Fisher by park commissioner Calvin Sommer. The facility housed a horticulture library, gift shop, workshop, and meeting space. It also provided an interior space for gardening and craft classes and horticulture workshops. In March 1966, the Garden Center was renamed in honor of Fred W. Green, longtime advisor to the Garden Forum.

Fellows Riverside Gardens is known for its romantic rose garden, shown here prior to the construction of the South Terrace pavilion. Millions of visitors have made this a favorite destination in Mill Creek Park. For decades, wedding parties have experienced the roses' magnificent colors and alluring fragrance on their special day. (Courtesy of the *Vindicator*.)

A generous variety of trees and shrubs serves as the background for the many floral displays. Shade trees, flowering trees, and shrubs combine to create smaller gardens within a garden. Collections of European beeches, rhododendrons, hollies, shade plants, herbs, dwarf conifers, and perennials are displayed for the enjoyment of the visitor. This aerial view gives a commanding perspective of the Victorian Gazebo, the site for the perfect garden wedding. Designed by Robert Mastriana of the 4M Company, the gazebo was built in 1983 in memory of Mabel Snyder Beeghly.

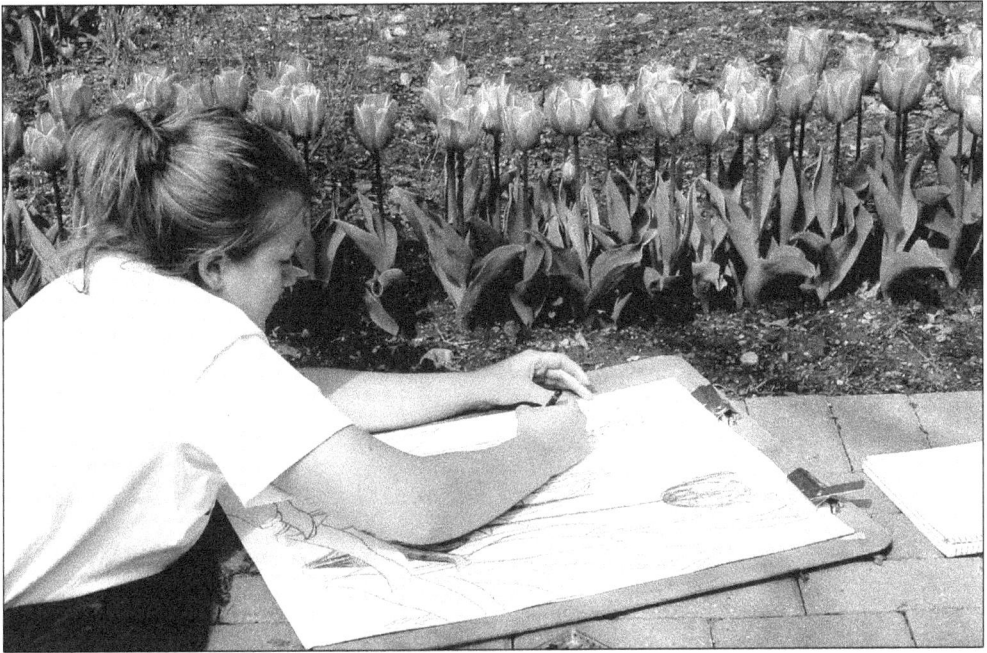

The beauty of the gardens draws artists, photographers, and home gardeners looking for inspiration. The remarkable landscape both entertains and enlightens through labeled plant collections and educational, cultural, and social activities. Horticulture classes attract students of all ages. Since Mill Creek Park's opening in 1891, millions of happy memories have been created at sites throughout the 2,600 acres of parklands.

Every year, 40,000 bulbs announce the arrival of spring. Crocus, tulip, and narcissus bulbs provide abundant color. Annuals by the thousands replace the spring bulbs and continue the show. An army of dedicated volunteers contributes countless hours to assist staff in the labor-intensive bulb planting. Residents and visitors from around the world come to the gardens to experience the beauty and splendor of the ever-changing colorful extravaganza.

In 1904, Volney Rogers wrote: "The advantages of public parks are many; but the greatest is their healthful, healing influence. . . . Cool, inviting shades and clear, still, or whispering waters; pure air, bright sunshine, and pastoral scenery are not only Nature's healing balms for bodily and mental afflictions, but they lead the appreciative mind and heart gently on, step by step, to the great lovable Truth."

·

www.ingramcontent.com/pod-product-compliance
Lightning Source LLC
Chambersburg PA
CBHW050633110426
42813CB00007B/1798